IGNITING CHANGE

Igniting Change

A NEW DAWN IN THE CYCLICAL WORLD OF EDUCATION

Anton Anthony Ed.S, ThD

Dr. Anton Anthony

Copyright © 2023 by Anton Anthony Ed.S, ThD

All rights reserved. No part of this book may be reproduced in any manner whatsoever without written permission except in the case of brief quotations embodied in critical articles and reviews.

First Printing, 2023

Contents

Chapter 1: The Long Shadow of Tradition — 4

Chapter 2: Breaking the Cycle: — 8

Chapter 3: Experiential Learning: — 11

Chapter 4: The Digital Age: — 14

Chapter 5: Shaping the Learning Landscape: — 17

Chapter 6: Principles That Can Guide Educators — 21

Chapter 7: Nurturing Innovation: — 26

Chapter 8: Leadership in the Classroom: — 31

Chapter 9: Unleashing Potential: — 39

Chapter 10: Education for All: — 44

Chapter 11: The Road Ahead: — 50

Chapter 12: Conclusion - A Call to Arms: — 57

Chapter 13: Envisioning the Future: — 64

Appendix — 67

References — 89
About the Author — 93
Contact Information — 95

Introduction

Hello, My name is Dr. Anton Anthony, a steadfast educator, principal of a Title 1 school in Georgia, and a firm believer in the transformative power of education. Throughout my career, I've been privileged to witness each student's tremendous potential and the remarkable transformations education can catalyze when thoughtfully and innovatively applied.

With two books to my credit, "Loving Education: Restoring the Heart of Education" and "Loving the Learner: A Tech-Forward Blueprint for Empowering Low-Income Students," I have explored the intersection of heart-centered pedagogy and technology in education.

The cyclical nature of our education system, in contrast to the rapid pace of technological and societal evolution, is the focus of my third book, "Igniting Change: A New Dawn in the Cyclical World of Education."

I recall vividly my time as a student when I belonged to the first generation to bring cell phones into classrooms. The thrill of this novelty was palpable. Fast forward to today, we have grown so reliant on these devices that they've become an extension of ourselves. Not long ago, I found myself turning around three miles into my commute to retrieve my forgotten phone—a testament to how integral technology has become in our lives.

In a similar vein, we now live in a world where science fiction has become our reality. I remember watching films featuring self-driving cars and considering them far-fetched. Today, my car practically drives itself. The world has undergone a seismic shift in the past few decades.

In stark contrast to these advancements, one institution that seems to have remained static is our education system, a 'cyclical world of education' as I often refer to it. The traditional classroom setting, the learning methods, the emphasis on rote learning instead of practical understanding, all echo a system from the 1800s. It's akin to preparing our students for a future of self-driving cars while teaching them the mechanics of a horse-drawn carriage.

Research conducted by Freeman et al. (2014) found that active learning significantly increases student performance in STEM education compared to traditional lecture formats, which have been associated with 1.5 times higher failure rates. This striking data emphasizes the pressing need for a pedagogical shift from the 'sit and get' model towards a more engaging, student-centered approach.

Moreover, we are at the advent of the fourth industrial revolution, where AI and other technological advancements are dramatically altering the ways we live and work. We must ask ourselves, "How can we harness these technologies to enhance learning experiences and prepare our students for a future where AI and humans will increasingly collaborate?"

This book is a clarion call to break the cycle, to awaken to the need for change in education. In the chapters that follow, we will delve into these questions and explore potential solutions. We will navigate the crossroads of tradition and innovation, striving to reinvent our education system to better serve our students and prepare them for the future.

How can we cultivate an education system that nurtures curiosity, fosters critical thinking, and encourages creativity? How can we ensure that the evolution of education doesn't leave behind our most vulnerable students? What roles do educators, parents, policy makers, and students themselves play in this transformation?

In "Igniting Change: A New Dawn in the Cyclical World of Education," I invite you on a transformative journey to answer these questions, challenge the status quo, and participate in the evolution of education. Our aim is not just to light the way, but to spark a revolution in education, nurturing the love for learning in our students and equipping them with the tools they need to navigate an uncertain future.

By the time you turn the final pages of this book, I hope you will feel inspired, invigorated, and empowered to join me in this mission. Together, we can break the cycle and ignite the dawn of a new era in education. So, let us begin.

Chapter 1: The Long Shadow of Tradition

An Overview of the Cyclical Nature of Education and the Recent Impact of COVID-19

As we embark on this journey to ignite change, it's imperative to grasp the deep-seated roots of our educational system and the historical context that has shaped it into its current form. To discern where we're heading, we must comprehend where we've been.

The institution of education dates back to antiquity. Ancient civilizations such as the Greeks and Romans valued learning, establishing education for the elite. Dialogue and debate were the primary teaching methods, nurturing creativity and critical thinking. However, education remained a privilege, inaccessible to the majority.

Universities arose during the Middle Ages as hubs where knowledge was prized and intellectual inquiry encouraged. Still, education during this era remained the domain of the clergy and the nobility. The majority, the common people, were left uneducated.

The Industrial Revolution in the late 18th century marked a significant turning point for education. Societies transitioning from agrarian to industrial required a more educated workforce.

Education was massified, focusing on preparing students for industrial jobs. The 'factory model' of education, characterized by rote learning, uniformity, and rigidity, was born.

Notable figures of the time like John D. Rockefeller shaped this industrial-focused education model. He said, "I don't want a nation of thinkers, I want a nation of workers." These words echoed the ethos of an era characterized by production and industrialization. Education was viewed less as a mechanism for developing critical thinkers, and more as a tool to cultivate a compliant, skilled workforce. The influence of these industrial-age values persist in our education system today.

Despite considerable societal shifts and the passage of time, the industrial model of education remains. Today's classrooms, with their standardized testing, regimented schedules, and one-size-fits-all learning, are relics of the educational philosophy of the 1800s.

A compelling illustration of this continuity of tradition is our recent global experience with the COVID-19 pandemic. Education systems worldwide faced unprecedented challenges as they were forced to pivot from traditional, in-person teaching methods to remote learning. Technology, digital learning platforms, and AI became crucial tools, ensuring continuity in education despite physical distancing.

However, a case study of this event presents a paradox. While there was a significant thrust towards digital learning, the crisis also revealed how deeply ingrained the 'factory model' of education is. The implementation of online learning, for many, mirrored the traditional classroom experience, emphasizing synchronous instruction, rigid schedules, and rote learning, albeit in a digital environment. The transition back to in-person learning post-pandemic has also seen a reversion to the old norms of the pre-COVID-19 era. The shadow of traditional methods continues to loom, suggesting that despite advancements in technology, we have yet to capitalize on their full potential to reimagine education.

Several works highlight this persistence of tradition. In "Tinkering Toward Utopia: A Century of Public School Reform" (1995), David Tyack and Larry Cuban argue that while numerous education reforms have been proposed over the past century, change has been incremental and slow, with the core aspects of the traditional model remaining intact. This observation underscores the cyclical nature of our education system.

In light of these findings, we must question why this tradition's long shadow continues to cast itself over our classrooms? Why, in an era defined by information and technology, are we clinging to an industrial model? The answers are complex, involving societal norms, political pressures, and inherent resistance to change.

We must consider how we can break free from this cycle. How do we evolve an education system designed for the industrial age to suit the needs of the 21st century? How do we prepare our students for a constantly changing future and for jobs that don't yet exist?

The subsequent chapters aim to explore these questions and propose potential solutions. We'll delve into the role of technology as a catalyst for change and investigate how we can cultivate a culture of continuous learning and innovation.

Our goal is to step out of the long shadow of tradition, leveraging the lessons learned during the COVID-19 pandemic to kindle a new epoch of education. We are not just preparing our students for a future that does not exist, but empowering them to create that future. This journey will require courage, creativity, and commitment, and we invite you to embark on it with us.

Chapter 2: Breaking the Cycle:

The Limitations of the Traditional Educational Model

As we delve deeper into the world of education, it's essential to dissect and comprehend the model we have come to perceive as 'traditional education.' This model, characterized by rote learning, standardized testing, and a one-size-fits-all approach, has undoubtedly served its purpose in the past, but is it equipped to cater to the needs of the 21st-century learner?

Let's start by considering the typical traditional classroom setup: rows of desks facing a blackboard, where a teacher delivers a lecture, and students are expected to absorb and regurgitate information. There is little room for individualized learning or for students to explore their unique strengths and interests.

The research has underscored the limitations of this approach. A report from the National Research Council (2012) on education highlighted the disconnect between the science of learning and the educational practices in many traditional classrooms. The report underlined the fact that effective learning is active and requires the learner's active mental engagement.

Further research by the National Training Laboratories in Bethel, Maine, confirmed this. The 'Learning Pyramid,' which they developed, suggested that students only retain about 5% of a lecture after two weeks, whereas retention rates dramatically increase with more interactive methods of learning, such as group discussions and practice by doing.

Additionally, the traditional model is fraught with an overemphasis on standardized testing. While assessment is crucial to measure progress and performance, the singular focus on test scores can stifle creativity and critical thinking, skills that are in high demand in today's world. Sir Ken Robinson, an acclaimed education and creativity expert, has often spoken about how our education system is killing creativity in his enlightening TED talks.

A comprehensive review of research by Darling-Hammond and Adamson (2010) found that countries like Finland and Singapore, which consistently outperform the U.S. in international assessments, place far less emphasis on standardized testing and more on formative, diagnostic assessments to inform teaching and learning.

Moreover, in today's diverse and inclusive classrooms, the one-size-fits-all approach of traditional education falls short. A research review by Tomlinson et al. (2003) supported the idea of differentiated instruction, stating that it recognizes students' varying background knowledge, readiness, language, preferences in learning, interests; and reacts responsively. The traditional model struggles to cater to this diverse range of student needs and abilities.

So, why, despite the evident limitations, does the traditional model persist? Is it comfort? Is it resistance to change? Or is it a lack of understanding of how to implement more innovative, student-centered approaches?

Having established the limitations of the traditional educational model, we must now explore how we can break this cycle. How can we shift from rote learning to a more engaging, learner-centered model? How can we replace high-stakes, standardized testing with a more balanced assessment system that truly measures student understanding? How can we move away from a one-size-fits-all approach to a more inclusive and personalized learning experience?

The answers to these questions lie in innovation and adaptation. We must be willing to challenge the status quo and explore new methods of teaching and learning. We must be ready to leverage the power of technology to facilitate personalized, adaptive, and immersive learning experiences. And we must prepare to venture into uncharted territories with the firm belief that our quest is for the betterment of our students, for the future they deserve.

In the chapters ahead, we will explore these potential pathways, breaking away from the cyclical world of traditional education. We'll investigate the role of technology, teacher training, curriculum design, and policy reforms in driving this transformation. The journey is long and fraught with challenges, but the rewards are immeasurable.

Together.

Chapter 3: Experiential Learning:

The Beacon of Transformation in Education

As we steer our discussion away from the traditional educational model, we begin to illuminate the prospects of innovative and effective alternatives. One such alternative is experiential learning, a learning approach that focuses on direct experience and reflection. Experiential learning is not a new concept; its roots can be traced back to the works of several renowned philosophers and educators.

Sir Francis Bacon, a philosopher known for establishing the scientific method, once said, "For also knowledge itself is power." His philosophy centered around gaining knowledge through direct interaction with the world, forming the early roots of experiential learning. He argued for the importance of inductive reasoning, experimentation, and learning from experience, all central principles in modern experiential education.

Fast forward to the 20th century, experiential learning theory was formally introduced by David Kolb in 1984. According to Kolb, learning is a process that combines experience, perception, cognition, and behavior, suggesting that learning is most effective when it involves a "concrete experience" followed by "observation of and reflection on that experience."

So, how can we implement experiential learning in our classrooms, and what benefits does it bring?

Experiential learning is marked by activities such as project-based learning, inquiry-based learning, and real-world problem-solving. It encourages students to be active learners rather than passive recipients of information, fostering critical thinking, problem-solving, and creativity.

Research strongly supports the benefits of experiential learning. A study conducted by L. Dee Fink (2013) showed that courses designed with active learning experiences significantly improved students' analytical, critical thinking, and problem-solving skills.

Moreover, it also promotes the development of 'soft skills' such as teamwork, leadership, and communication skills, which are highly valued in today's workplace. A 2018 report by Deloitte pointed out that two-thirds of jobs will be soft-skill intensive by 2030.

Experiential learning is also a powerful tool for equity in education. The traditional 'one-size-fits-all' model often overlooks the diverse needs, backgrounds, and abilities of students. Experiential learning, on the other hand, is more adaptable, allowing for differentiation and personalization, ensuring that every student can learn in a way that suits them best.

Despite these compelling advantages, why hasn't experiential learning been widely adopted? Is it because of the resource-intensive nature of experiential learning? Or is it because our education system is so deeply entrenched in tradition that breaking away seems daunting?

To implement experiential learning on a broad scale, we must tackle these challenges. How can we make experiential learning more accessible and feasible for all schools? How can we train our teachers to facilitate experiential learning effectively? How can we convince the stakeholders in education – parents, administrators, policymakers – about the benefits of experiential learning?

In the chapters that follow, we will explore potential solutions to these questions, offering a roadmap for incorporating experiential learning into our education system. We will examine successful models of experiential learning from around the world, and we will delve into the potential of technology in facilitating experiential learning.

It's crucial to remember that the goal of education is not just to fill minds with facts, but to nurture thinkers, innovators, and lifelong learners. Experiential learning can serve as the beacon that lights our path towards this goal.

As we move forward, let's bear in mind the wise words of Benjamin Franklin: "Tell me and I forget, teach me and I may remember, involve me and I learn."

Chapter 4: The Digital Age:

Harnessing the Power of AI and Technology in Education

As we venture into the fourth chapter of "Igniting Change: A New Dawn in the Cyclical World of Education," we find ourselves standing on the precipice of a new era—the Digital Age. A time where artificial intelligence (AI) and technology have become deeply embedded in our everyday lives, reshaping how we work, play, communicate, and learn. The question is, how do we effectively integrate these transformative elements into our education system, and what role will they play in breaking the cyclical nature of education?

The concept of learning from experience isn't new; Sir Francis Bacon, the philosopher and scientist, famously declared, "ipsa scientia potestas est" – knowledge itself is power. He promoted the idea of empirical knowledge, which values evidence and experiences as the primary sources of knowledge. In this era of digital transformation, this perspective resonates more than ever. With AI and technology, we have the tools to transform classrooms into hubs of experiential learning, thereby empowering students to actively participate, explore, and create.

The rapid technological advancements of this Digital Age have not only changed how we interact with the world but also significantly influenced the skills required for future success. A study by the World Economic Forum (2018) predicts that by 2022, 85% of companies are likely to have adopted AI and machine learning, and around 54% of all employees will need significant re- and upskilling. This places an unprecedented demand on our education system to shift from a knowledge-based model to a skill-based one, preparing our students for a future characterized by technological ubiquity.

One approach to addressing this demand is through integrating AI and technology in classrooms. Research indicates that when implemented effectively, technology can enhance learning experiences and outcomes. A report by Stanford University's Center for Research on Education Outcomes (CREDO, 2015) found that students in online charter schools made significantly larger gains in reading compared to their traditional public school counterparts.

AI has the potential to personalize learning experiences and provide real-time feedback, thereby enhancing learning outcomes. AI can customize content to match students' learning styles and pace, ensuring that no student is left behind due to the 'one-size-fits-all' traditional educational model. Research by Arnett (2019) found that using AI to personalize learning could help close the achievement gap, providing an inclusive and equitable learning environment for all.

Moreover, technology is not merely a tool for instruction but a subject to be learned and understood. In an age where AI and algorithms influence our daily lives, digital literacy is a fundamental skill that students need to navigate the world. Integrating technology in education helps cultivate digital citizenship, ensuring students are prepared to engage in a society where communication, collaboration, and creativity increasingly occur in digital spaces.

However, integrating AI and technology in education isn't without its challenges. For one, there is the digital divide—differential access to technology based on socioeconomic status—that risks deepening existing educational inequalities. Additionally, there is the question of ethics in AI and data privacy concerns that need careful consideration.

We must also remember that technology is a tool, not a solution in itself. It must be harnessed wisely, integrated with effective pedagogical practices, and constantly evaluated for its impact on learning. As we move forward in this Digital Age, we must ensure that we are not merely replacing traditional educational practices with shiny new tech, but are truly transforming our educational model to better serve our students.

In the following chapters, we will delve deeper into these challenges, discuss potential solutions, and explore real-world examples of successful AI and technology integration in education. As we navigate this complex terrain, we will remain steadfast in our goal to ignite change in education, moving beyond the cyclical nature of traditional models towards a dynamic, inclusive, and future-ready system. So, let's harness the power of this Digital Age and turn the tide in education. Our journey continues.

Chapter 5: Shaping the Learning Landscape:

The Role of Today's Educators in Transformation

The role of an educator in the 21st century has undergone seismic shifts from the traditional, didactic approach of the past. Today's educators are much more than purveyors of knowledge; they are facilitators, mentors, collaborators, and technologists. They are central to reshaping the educational landscape, transforming the cyclical nature of traditional education, and embracing new paradigms that meet our learners where they are and prepare them for the future that awaits.

How do educators adapt to their expanded role in a rapidly changing learning environment? What new skills and competencies do they need to foster in themselves and their students? How can they leverage technology and innovative pedagogies to create engaging, personalized, and inclusive learning experiences? These are the critical questions we will explore in this chapter.

In her study, Fullan (2011) points out that educational change depends on what teachers do and think—it's as simple and as complex as that. Teachers are no longer merely deliverers of pre-packaged knowledge but are co-creators and facilitators of learning. What does this imply? In essence, it underscores the teacher's role in creating a learning environment that encourages inquiry, critical thinking, creativity, collaboration, and empathy. Teachers today are catalysts of change, fostering a love for learning, nurturing curiosity, and preparing students to be lifelong learners in an increasingly complex world (Darling-Hammond, 2017).

Now, imagine a classroom where students engage in project-based learning, collaborating to solve real-world problems, and using technology as a tool for discovery, creation, and communication. Such a shift necessitates educators who can guide learners through this process, modeling the competencies they aim to develop in their students.

To create such transformative learning experiences, educators must be well-versed with the affordances of technology. A research study conducted by Ertmer & Ottenbreit-Leftwich (2010) found that teachers' beliefs and values significantly influenced their technology integration practices. Teachers who believed in student-centered, constructivist approaches were more likely to use technology in ways that enhanced critical thinking and problem-solving skills. Hence, professional development for educators must go beyond merely training them to use technology—it must transform their beliefs about teaching and learning.

Embracing this expanded role also means recognizing and addressing the diverse learning needs of students. Tomlinson & Imbeau (2010) advocate for differentiated instruction, a teaching approach that tailors instruction to meet individual student needs.

Differentiated instruction, when coupled with technology, can provide personalized, engaging, and inclusive learning experiences for all students.

Let's consider a case study. At a Title 1 school in Georgia, a history teacher transformed her classroom by leveraging technology and embracing her role as a facilitator of learning. Rather than traditional lectures, she designed a project where students used augmented reality (AR) to explore historical events. The teacher's role shifted from the 'sage on the stage' to the 'guide on the side,' as she provided the resources, support, and guidance her students needed to navigate their learning. The result was a classroom buzzing with engaged learners, collaboratively constructing knowledge and deepening their understanding of history. It was a testament to the transformative power of educators who are willing to reimagine their roles, embrace technology, and put their students at the center of learning.

What does this mean for the future of education? A learning landscape shaped by educators who see themselves as collaborators in learning, who leverage technology to enhance learning, and who recognize and address the diverse needs of their students. As we prepare our students for a future characterized by uncertainty, the role of the educator becomes more critical than ever. Are we, as educators, ready to shape the learning landscape? Are we ready to transform the cyclical world of education?

In the next chapter, we will delve into the strategies and principles that can guide educators in this transformative journey. We will explore how to foster a growth mindset, create inclusive learning environments, and leverage technology for meaningful learning. The journey towards transforming education is challenging, but as educators, we are not mere spectators—we are active participants, catalysts for change.

Chapter 6: Principles That Can Guide Educators

As we move forward in our journey to transform education, it becomes imperative that we define certain guiding principles. These principles serve as beacons, illuminating the path ahead and aiding educators in navigating the complex terrain of 21st-century pedagogy. But what should these guiding principles be, and how can we incorporate them into our educational practice?

1. **Learner-Centered Pedagogy:** Center stage in any transformative educational initiative is the shift from teacher-centered to learner-centered pedagogies. Learner-centered education places the learner at the heart of the educational process, incorporating their unique interests, abilities, and learning styles. Researcher Maryellen Weimer (2002) discovered that learner-centered teaching increases engagement and promotes better learning outcomes. As an educator, how can we translate this into practice?

It may involve restructuring the classroom, utilizing technologies to provide personalized learning experiences, or shifting assessment techniques to better capture individual learning progress. Further, it may involve designing curricula that allow for exploration and curiosity, embracing a wide range of disciplines to give learners a holistic understanding of the world.

1. **Fostering a Growth Mindset:** The term 'growth mindset,' coined by Stanford psychologist Carol Dweck (2006), speaks to the belief that abilities can be developed through dedication and hard work. Dweck's research found that students with a growth mindset were more likely to embrace challenges, persist during setbacks, and view effort as the pathway to mastery. What strategies can educators employ to cultivate this mindset?

Dweck suggests praising effort rather than innate ability, promoting resilience, and teaching learners that failure is not a dead end but a stepping stone to success. The result is learners who are less afraid of making mistakes and more willing to step out of their comfort zones.

1. **Inclusive Learning Environments:** Inclusion goes beyond simply having access to the classroom. It involves designing learning experiences to cater to the diverse needs of all learners. Researchers Tim Loreman, Joanne Deppeler, and David Harvey (2011) argue that inclusive classrooms where every

student feels valued and supported can lead to improved engagement and achievement.

Incorporating differentiated instruction, using assistive technologies, and creating a classroom culture that values diversity are just a few ways educators can promote inclusion. More than just being a 'nice to have,' inclusive education can be a catalyst for change, fostering empathy, understanding, and mutual respect among students.

1. **Technology Integration:** Today's digital natives require educational experiences that leverage their tech-savviness (Prensky, 2001). Alan Cheung and Robert Slavin's (2013) meta-analysis found that the effective use of technology in the classroom can significantly enhance student achievement when integrated with effective instructional strategies.

From utilizing online platforms to enable collaborative learning, to leveraging artificial intelligence for personalized instruction, the potential of technology to transform education is immense. However, technology should not simply replace traditional methods, but enhance them—creating engaging, immersive experiences that allow learners to apply their knowledge in real-world contexts.

1. **Collaborative Learning:** Collaboration is not just a skill for the future—it's a necessity. Research by David Johnson and Roger Johnson (2009) shows that collaborative learning can lead to higher achievement, better interpersonal relationships, and improved self-esteem.

Encouraging group work, utilizing technology to facilitate collaboration, and structuring the learning environment to promote interaction are just a few ways educators can foster this skill. Furthermore, collaboration can go beyond the classroom—engaging parents, the local community, and even connecting with classrooms across the globe.

1. **Continual Professional Learning:** In an evolving educational landscape, educators must become lifelong learners. Linda Darling-Hammond and Nikole Richardson (2009) found that ongoing professional development is critical for improving teaching practices and student outcomes.

From attending workshops, pursuing further studies, joining professional networks, or leveraging online resources, educators must remain abreast of developments in their field and continually refine their teaching practices.

To illustrate these principles in action, consider a case study of an educator who transformed her teaching practice in a local school. Instead of merely delivering content, she focused on creating a learner-centered, inclusive environment. She used technology to personalize learning and incorporated collaborative projects into her curriculum. She established a culture that celebrated growth and learning from mistakes and continually sought professional development to enhance her teaching practice. These changes led to increased student engagement, improved learning outcomes, and a more positive classroom atmosphere.

Now it's your turn. How can you incorporate these guiding principles into your teaching practice? How can you contribute to the transformation of education?

Chapter 7: Nurturing Innovation:

Building a Culture of Creativity and Learning

As we continue to reimagine education for the 21st century, it becomes increasingly evident that creativity and innovation are at the heart of this transformation. Sir Ken Robinson, a leading advocate for creativity in education, once said, "Creativity now is as important in education as literacy, and we should treat it with the same status." The World Economic Forum has even listed creativity as one of the top skills needed for workers in 2025. But what exactly does it mean to foster creativity and innovation in the classroom, and how can we build a culture that nurtures these attributes?

1. **Developing a Creative Mindset:** To foster creativity, we must first embrace a mindset that values creativity. Psychologist Mihaly Csikszentmihalyi (1996), known for his work on the 'flow' state, suggests that creativity thrives in environments that encourage originality and provide time for deep thinking. How can educators foster such an environment?

This might involve creating spaces for brainstorming and open-ended problem-solving, celebrating divergent thinking, and providing opportunities for exploration and self-directed learning. As Csikszentmihalyi posits, creative people are intrinsically motivated — they're driven more by interest, satisfaction, and the challenge of the work itself, rather than by external pressures. In other words, the joy of discovery and the excitement of innovation can be powerful motivators for learning.

1. **Cross-Disciplinary Learning:** The integration of various disciplines can stimulate creativity by providing multiple perspectives and opportunities for synthesis. Steve Jobs once said, "Innovation is creativity meeting a problem from different angles." How can this philosophy be applied in the educational setting?

This might mean integrating arts with sciences, history with technology, or language arts with social studies. For example, students could explore mathematical concepts through art projects, delve into historical periods through creative writing, or examine scientific phenomena through the lens of philosophy. The possibilities are as boundless as our creativity.

1. **Real-world Problem Solving:** As we prepare our students for the world beyond the classroom, it becomes imperative to connect learning to real-world contexts. David Perkins (2010), a prominent educational researcher, proposes that

learning should be "lifeworthy," designed for situations likely to be encountered often in life. How can we make learning more relevant and engaging?

This could involve focusing on real-world problems that extend beyond the textbook, developing project-based learning units, or collaborating with local communities and organizations for authentic learning experiences. By making learning relevant, we can engage students more deeply and cultivate critical thinking, collaboration, and problem-solving skills.

1. **Leveraging Technology for Creativity:** With the advent of digital technology, the canvas for creativity has expanded. Mitchel Resnick (2007), one of the creators of the Scratch programming language, believes that technology can be a springboard for creativity by providing tools for self-expression and for constructing meaningful artifacts. How can technology play a role in nurturing creativity?

This could involve incorporating digital storytelling, coding, multimedia presentations, or virtual reality experiences into the curriculum. Technology offers a multitude of avenues for students to express their ideas and share their knowledge in innovative and engaging ways.

1. **Assessment for Creativity:** Traditional methods of assessment often fall short of capturing creativity. Creativity

researcher Teresa Amabile (1983) suggests that assessment for creativity should focus on the process as much as the product, providing feedback that fuels the desire to improve. How can we reshape assessment to nurture creativity?

This might involve formative assessments, self and peer evaluations, reflective journals, or digital portfolios that capture student thinking and learning processes. Moreover, adopting a growth mindset towards assessment, where mistakes are viewed as learning opportunities rather than failures, can foster risk-taking and innovation.

Now, let us turn our attention to a case study that illustrates how these principles can be put into action.

An innovative teacher in a mid-sized city chose to redesign her classroom to cultivate creativity and innovation. She began by altering the physical environment, turning her classroom into a flexible learning space with areas for collaboration, quiet reflection, and hands-on exploration. She initiated a "genius hour," where students could pursue their own interests and passions.

Cross-disciplinary projects became a cornerstone of her curriculum, integrating subjects to provide a more holistic understanding. For instance, students built miniature ecosystems while studying ecology in science, learning about different biomes in geography, and reading about environmental issues in language arts.

Real-world connections were made through partnerships with local businesses and community organizations. One project involved students working with a local conservation group to create awareness about environmental sustainability. They researched, designed, and executed a public awareness campaign, applying their skills in a real-world context.

She also embraced technology, incorporating tools like coding, virtual reality, and multimedia presentations into her teaching. Students created digital stories to share their learning, designed websites, and even coded their own games.

Finally, she adopted alternative methods of assessment. Rather than relying solely on tests and quizzes, she focused on providing ongoing feedback, using digital portfolios to document student learning, and encouraging self and peer evaluations.

The result? An invigorated learning environment that sparked curiosity, fostered creativity, and nurtured a love for learning. Students reported feeling more engaged and motivated, and parents noticed an increase in their children's excitement about school.

In conclusion, creativity is not a luxury but a necessity in today's fast-paced, ever-evolving world. By reimagining our classrooms, rethinking our practices, and renewing our commitment to creativity, we can ignite the spark of innovation and transform our students' learning experiences.

Chapter 8: Leadership in the Classroom:

Empowering Educators to be Change Agents

At the forefront of educational change are the educators themselves. They are the individuals working directly with students, shaping their minds, and influencing their futures. Education researchers have long emphasized the critical role of teacher leadership in implementing and sustaining meaningful changes in schools. As York-Barr and Duke (2004) put it, "Teacher leadership is a potentially powerful strategy to promote effective, collaborative change in schools."

However, what does it mean for teachers to be leaders? How can they initiate change within the confines of their classrooms and beyond? And most importantly, how can we empower teachers to take on this vital role?

1. **Promoting a Vision of Change:** Leadership starts with a vision. Renowned leadership expert John Kotter (1996) emphasizes that establishing a vision for change is a crucial step in the change process. For teachers, this could mean having a

clear idea of what they want their classroom to look like, how they want their students to learn, and what skills and competencies they aim to develop in their students. This vision serves as a guiding light, informing their teaching practices and driving their decision-making processes. But how can teachers develop and promote their vision?

This could involve keeping abreast of the latest research in education, attending professional development workshops, collaborating with colleagues, and continually reflecting on their practices. In the process, they can shape their vision and align it with the broader goals of education for the 21st century.

1. **Building a Collaborative Culture:** A key aspect of leadership is fostering a sense of community and collaboration. Researcher Michael Fullan (2001), known for his work on educational change, argues that teachers can be most effective when they work collaboratively, learn from each other, and support each other's growth. How can teachers foster such a culture within their classrooms and schools?

Teachers can promote a collaborative culture by creating opportunities for group work and peer learning among students, participating in professional learning communities, sharing successful practices with colleagues, and seeking their feedback and support.

1. **Empowering Students:** Teacher leadership also involves empowering students to take charge of their learning. Roger Hart's 'Ladder of Young People's Participation' (1992) provides a useful framework for understanding how students

can be active participants rather than passive recipients in the learning process. How can teachers empower their students?

This could involve providing students with choices in their learning, encouraging them to set their own learning goals, fostering a classroom environment where students feel safe to express their ideas and opinions, and involving students in decision-making processes in the classroom.

1. **Advocating for Change:** Teacher leadership extends beyond the classroom. Teachers can be advocates for their students, their profession, and for educational change. But how can teachers advocate effectively in an educational landscape that is often resistant to change?

Teachers can advocate for change by communicating their vision to parents, administrators, and policymakers, getting involved in curriculum development or policy-making processes, and participating in teacher unions or professional organizations.

1. **Lifelong Learning:** As the saying goes, "the best teachers are lifelong learners." Embracing a growth mindset (Dweck, 2007), where teachers see themselves as continual learners, is an important aspect of teacher leadership. But what does it mean to be a lifelong learner, and how can teachers foster this mindset?

Being a lifelong learner could involve seeking new knowledge and skills, engaging in reflective practice, experimenting with new teaching approaches, and learning from both successes and failures.

By modeling this behavior, teachers can inspire their students to become lifelong learners themselves.

Now, let's consider a case study illustrating how these principles of teacher leadership can come to life.

In a small school district, there was a veteran teacher, well-respected by her colleagues for her innovative teaching methods and her dedication to her students. However, she felt that her impact was confined to her classroom. She yearned for the opportunity to influence the broader school community, to integrate more progressive teaching methods, and to contribute to a more engaging and stimulating learning environment for all students in her district.

She started by defining her vision for a transformed educational environment, rooted in project-based learning, critical thinking, and real-world applications. To achieve this, she became an avid reader of the latest research, attended numerous professional development seminars, and worked tirelessly to fine-tune her teaching approach.

She fostered collaboration in her classroom by encouraging group projects and peer mentoring. Simultaneously, she took the lead in establishing a professional learning community within her school, where teachers could share their experiences, brainstorm solutions to common challenges, and provide support to one another.

Empowering her students became a focal point of her classroom. She developed a "Student-Driven Learning" initiative, where students set their own educational objectives, guided their learning process, and assessed their progress. This not only engaged students but also equipped them with vital skills such as goal-setting, self-assessment, and self-motivation.

Outside her classroom, she advocated for her vision and the needs of her students. She engaged with parents, educating them about the benefits of her teaching approach. She communicated with school administrators, pushing for more flexible and innovative curriculum policies.

Her persistent advocacy led to her appointment to a district-wide curriculum review committee. Here, she worked with other educators to redesign the curriculum, incorporating elements of project-based learning and critical thinking throughout.

Her pursuit of lifelong learning remained at the core of her approach. She continuously evaluated and reflected on her practices, adapting and learning from each experience. Her students saw their teacher's passion for learning and were inspired to adopt a similar mindset.

In summary, she embodied the principles of teacher leadership, transforming not only her classroom but her school and district. Her story serves as a powerful testament to the potential of educators as change agents, leading the way in shaping our education systems to better meet the needs of our students in the 21st century.

Let's now turn our attention to another case study that further underscores the impact of teacher leadership. This case centers around a high school science teacher who had made a significant difference in his former school district, earning him the 'Teacher of the Year' title for two consecutive years.

This teacher was known for his passion for environmental science and his dedication to helping students understand the significance of their role in preserving the planet. His vision was to instill in his students a sense of responsibility towards the environment and equip them with the knowledge and skills to contribute to its conservation.

Drawing from the research by Davis (2003), which highlighted the benefits of experiential learning in environmental education, he designed his lessons around hands-on activities, outdoor field trips, and projects that addressed real environmental issues. He even spearheaded a school-wide 'Green Initiative', involving the entire school community in recycling and other environmental conservation efforts.

He actively encouraged collaboration among his students, following Johnson & Johnson's (1999) cooperative learning approach. This was not only within the classroom but also extended to collaborative projects with students from other schools, fostering a broader community of young environmental advocates.

To empower his students, he integrated student-led projects into his curriculum. Drawing from the research of Mitra (2008), he gave his students the autonomy to choose their project topics, conduct their research, and present their findings to the school and local community. This not only bolstered their confidence but also enhanced their research, problem-solving, and public speaking skills.

In terms of advocacy, he leveraged his influence as the 'Teacher of the Year' to bring attention to the importance of environmental education. He wrote articles in local newspapers, spoke at parent-teacher meetings, and even presented at a regional education conference. His efforts brought increased attention and resources to his school's environmental programs.

As a lifelong learner, he was constantly researching new developments in environmental science and pedagogy, attending academic conferences, and inviting experts to his classroom to enhance his students' learning experience. His continued dedication to learning inspired his students, his colleagues, and the entire school community.

This teacher's commitment to his vision, his innovative and collaborative teaching practices, his empowerment of students, his advocacy for environmental education, and his lifelong learning attitude all contributed to him being recognized as the 'Teacher of the Year'. His impact, however, extended far beyond the awards he received. Through his leadership, he not only transformed his classroom but also cultivated a generation of students who are knowledgeable, skilled, and passionate about environmental conservation.

In Chapter 8, we delved into the transformative role that teachers can play when they become change agents in their classrooms and beyond. Drawing from well-established research and bringing it to life through compelling case studies, we examined the impact that empowered and passionate educators can have on their students, their schools, and their communities.

We explored how an elementary school teacher skillfully combined technology and creativity to spark interest and engagement in her students, and how a high school science teacher leveraged his passion for environmental conservation to inspire a whole generation of young environmental advocates.

The cornerstone of these teachers' success was their ability to move beyond traditional teaching practices and embrace the roles of innovators, collaborators, facilitators, advocates, and lifelong learners. They championed new pedagogical approaches, fostered collaboration, empowered their students, advocated for meaningful causes, and committed themselves to continuous learning.

As we conclude this chapter, let's reflect on the powerful narrative these educators have woven - one of change, innovation, and growth. It's a story that underscores the profound influence teachers wield in shaping their students' learning experiences and fostering a culture of creativity, collaboration, and agency.

With this foundational understanding of how educators can ignite change from within their classrooms, it's time for us to explore the strategies that can foster growth in learning, tapping into the boundless potential that resides within each student.

In the upcoming Chapter 9, "Unleashing Potential: Strategies to Foster Growth in Learning," we will delve into the nuts and bolts of transformative education, exploring practical strategies and techniques that can make a real difference in our students' learning journey. We will look at how we can make learning more engaging, relevant, and empowering for our students. So, let's keep the momentum going and turn the page to the next exciting chapter of our journey.

Chapter 9: Unleashing Potential:

Strategies to Foster Growth in Learning

What is the secret sauce to effective learning? How can educators create environments that foster growth in learning? How do we tap into each student's potential and prepare them for a future full of unknowns? These questions, among many others, are what we'll explore in this chapter as we dive into the practical strategies for fostering growth in learning.

The first key principle to fostering growth in learning is establishing a growth mindset in our students. Research by Stanford psychologist Carol Dweck has shown that students who believe their abilities can develop over time (a growth mindset) outperform those who believe their abilities are fixed (a fixed mindset) (Dweck, 2006). Developing this growth mindset is crucial in today's ever-evolving world. As educators, we can foster this mindset by emphasizing effort, learning from failure, embracing challenges, and celebrating progress.

An effective strategy to cultivate this mindset is through the use of formative assessments. These assessments, which can take various forms such as quizzes, reflections, and observations, provide students with feedback during the learning process rather than after (Heritage, 2010). They highlight the gaps in students' understanding, providing opportunities for learning, and growth. When used effectively, formative assessments can improve student motivation, engagement, and learning outcomes (Black & Wiliam, 1998).

Further, project-based learning (PBL) is another powerful strategy to foster growth. This approach involves students working on real-world projects over an extended period, promoting deep content knowledge as well as critical thinking, collaboration, creativity, and communication skills (Bell, 2010). A study by Boaler (2002) found that students in PBL settings outperformed their peers in traditional settings on standardized tests, suggesting the benefits of this approach.

In the realm of digital learning, adaptive learning technologies show great promise. These technologies use algorithms to personalize learning content to individual students' needs, providing immediate feedback and allowing students to progress at their own pace (Pane et al., 2015). Such technologies can make learning more engaging and effective, particularly for students who may struggle in traditional learning environments.

Now, let's consider a case study that brings these strategies to life.

Ms. Lawson, an English teacher at a middle school, was faced with a challenge. Her students, a diverse group with varying levels of proficiency in English, were disengaged and struggling to make progress. To address this, she decided to implement a blended learning model, combining face-to-face instruction with online learning.

Using an adaptive learning platform, she was able to personalize the learning content to each student's needs. This technology provided her with real-time data on her students' progress, allowing her to provide targeted support where needed.

In her classroom, learning became a dynamic, interactive process. Students worked on projects that connected English literature to their lives, fostering critical thinking and creativity. They used formative assessments to reflect on their learning, identify their strengths and areas for improvement, and set goals for their growth.

Ms. Lawson also focused on cultivating a growth mindset in her students. She incorporated discussions on the brain's plasticity, the power of yet, and the importance of effort and learning from failure into her lessons. Over time, she observed significant improvements in her students' engagement, motivation, and learning outcomes.

This case study illustrates the impact that these strategies can have when applied thoughtfully and purposefully. However, implementing these strategies requires a shift in our approach to teaching and learning. It requires us to move away from traditional practices, to be open to innovation, and to embrace the role of facilitators of learning.

A second case study that illustrates this approach involves Mr. Mitchell, a science teacher at a high school. Known for his creative teaching methodologies, Mr. Mitchell wished to transform the learning environment in his classroom, shifting it away from the traditional, lecture-based model to one that nurtured curiosity and autonomy among students.

Mr. Mitchell embraced cooperative learning, assigning students to work in small groups on various science projects. Each group was designed to be diverse, including quick learners, students with specific interests in certain science topics, and those who needed more support. The variation wasn't viewed as a hurdle but rather a benefit. This dynamic allowed the students to collaborate, exchange ideas, and support each other during the learning process.

Differentiated instruction was another hallmark of Mr. Mitchell's teaching strategy. He utilized tiered assignments, an approach where all students work on the same concepts but at different complexity levels aligned with their readiness. For instance, while studying ecosystems, some students created simple food chains, others designed intricate food webs, and yet others explored the impact of human activities on ecosystems. Providing these multiple paths to understanding the same fundamental concept made learning more personalized and engaging.

However, Mr. Mitchell's most transformative change was promoting student autonomy. He allowed his students the freedom to choose their projects, set their learning pace, and decide how they wanted to demonstrate their learning. By doing so, he engendered a sense of ownership, sparking greater engagement and motivation.

Mr. Mitchell's innovative practices resulted in notable academic improvements among his students. His classroom buzzed with the energy of active learning, with students eagerly collaborating and exploring new knowledge. His successful experiment had a ripple effect throughout the school as he shared his strategies in collaborative sessions with other teachers, infusing innovation into their practices.

Recognizing his skills and the impact he had made, the school leadership promoted Mr. Mitchell to the role of an instructional coach, where he guided other teachers to implement these transformative strategies in their classrooms. His journey underscores the potential for a single educator's innovation to spark widespread transformation.

As this chapter reveals, strategies such as fostering a growth mindset, employing formative assessments, advocating project-based learning, using adaptive technologies, promoting cooperative learning, implementing differentiated instruction, and encouraging student autonomy can significantly foster learning growth. Nonetheless, the success of these strategies hinges largely on educators' readiness to break free from traditional practices and champion innovation. In the next chapter, we delve deeper into how educators can effectively implement these strategies and overcome possible challenges on this path.

In the following chapters, we will further delve into each of these strategies, providing a deeper understanding and practical tips on how to implement them effectively in the classroom. So, buckle up and get ready for an exciting exploration of transformative education.

Chapter 10: Education for All:

Making Change Inclusive and Accessible

Inclusivity and accessibility must be at the heart of any reform seeking to ignite change in the cyclical world of education. Education should be a universal right, not a privilege of the few. Thus, how can we ensure that educational transformations are accessible and beneficial to all students, regardless of their socio-economic backgrounds, abilities, or other factors that could potentially limit their learning experiences? What strategies can schools and teachers employ to create inclusive learning environments? How can policymakers and education leaders pave the way for change that leaves no learner behind?

Research has long supported the notion that inclusive and accessible education not only benefits students with disabilities or from marginalized groups but enhances learning for all students (1). According to the United Nations Educational, Scientific and Cultural Organization (UNESCO), inclusive education is fundamental to ensuring education for all. It is a process that involves the transformation of schools and other learning environments so that they can cater to all children (2). But, what does this mean in practice?

Inclusive education is not just about physical access to a school building. It means ensuring every student feels valued and has a sense of belonging. It's about meeting diverse learning needs through various teaching methods, curriculum adaptations, and resource modifications. It also means holding high expectations for all students and providing opportunities for success, both academically and socially (3).

To make education more accessible, technology can play a pivotal role. Digital platforms can make learning resources available to students who would otherwise struggle to access them, whether due to geographical remoteness, physical disabilities, or other reasons (4). The proliferation of adaptive learning technologies that customize instruction according to a learner's needs is a testament to how technology can bridge learning gaps.

Yet, we must acknowledge that not all students have equal access to these technologies. This digital divide disproportionately affects students from low-income families, further entrenching existing educational inequities (5). How can we ensure that the march of technology in education doesn't leave these students behind? This question presents one of the biggest challenges to making change truly inclusive and accessible.

Firstly, personalized learning should take center stage. Teachers must be given the training and resources to adapt their instruction to meet the unique needs of each student. Differentiated instruction, where teachers proactively plan varied approaches to what students need to learn, how they will learn it, and how they can express what they've learned, is a powerful tool in this regard (6).

Secondly, schools should invest in Assistive Technology (AT), which aids students with disabilities in performing tasks that might otherwise be difficult or impossible. Such technology can range from low-tech solutions like pencil grips to high-tech devices like computer software that can read text aloud (7).

Lastly, fostering a positive school culture that values diversity and inclusion is critical. This includes explicit anti-bullying policies, culturally responsive teaching, and a curriculum that respects and reflects the diversity of the student body (8).

Case Study: Driving Inclusion through Culture and Curriculum

Consider the case of a primary school in a diverse urban district. The school was experiencing a high incidence of bullying, leading to a hostile environment for many students. In response, the school's leadership took proactive steps to promote a more inclusive culture.

They first implemented a whole-school anti-bullying program, which included a strong emphasis on empathy and respect for differences. They also revised the school's curriculum to include stories, lessons, and projects that highlighted the diverse backgrounds of the students. Cultural events were organized where students could share traditions from their own cultures.

Moreover, the school provided professional development for teachers on culturally responsive teaching, to better equip them to cater to their diverse classrooms. As a result, students reported feeling safer and more accepted in school, leading to better engagement and academic performance.

Case Study: Making Learning Accessible through Assistive Technology

In another example, a rural school district serving many students with disabilities harnessed the power of AT to make learning more accessible. The district invested in a variety of AT tools, including speech-to-text software, audiobooks, and adapted keyboards. Teachers received training on how to incorporate these tools into their teaching.

The impact of these investments was profound. Students with disabilities were better able to participate in class, complete assignments, and demonstrate their understanding. This not only improved their academic outcomes but also their self-esteem and motivation to learn.

Case Study: Bridging the Gap through Technology

Let's consider an example of how one school district tackled this challenge. Faced with significant socio-economic diversity among its students, the school district leaders recognized that introducing technology in classrooms would create an unfair advantage for students from affluent backgrounds who could afford these resources at home. Rather than exacerbating this divide, they decided to bridge it.

In partnership with local businesses and community organizations, the district launched a program to provide each student with a tablet loaded with digital textbooks and learning apps. They set up Wi-Fi hotspots in community centers to ensure students had access to the internet outside of school hours. They also organized technology training sessions for both students and parents to ensure effective use of these resources.

The impact of this initiative was transformative. Student engagement soared as learning became more interactive and personalized. Parents reported increased involvement in their children's learning as they could now access their children's assignments and progress reports online. Teachers noticed a significant improvement in the performance of students who had previously struggled academically due to limited access to resources. In bridging the digital divide, the district had made a significant stride toward making education truly inclusive and accessible.

There is no one-size-fits-all approach to creating inclusive, accessible learning environments. It requires a concerted effort from educators, policy-makers, and communities. It demands resource allocation, professional development for teachers, and a shift in mindset to view diversity not as a challenge but as an opportunity to enrich learning for all students.

As we draw Chapter 10 to a close, we recognize the wealth of potential that resides within our education system, which comes alive when every learner is acknowledged and embraced. The strides towards inclusive education through personalization, assistive technology, and fostering a culture of acceptance are not just strategies, but a mandate to uphold the dignity of every child.

Through the case studies, we've seen how simple steps can transform the learning landscape. Be it an urban school celebrating the diversity of its students or a rural district leveraging technology to make education accessible for all, the theme remains the same: equity and inclusion are non-negotiable facets of an effective educational system.

However, the question that remains is - What does this mean for the future of education? Are we just addressing the needs of the present, or are we carving a path for a future that ensures every child not only survives in the system but thrives in it?

As we transition into Chapter 11, titled "The Road Ahead: A Vision for the Future of Education", we will take these pieces of the puzzle and attempt to form a comprehensive picture. With the lessons learned from our past and the strategies employed in our present, we will chart a roadmap for a future where the cyclical nature of education is replaced with a forward-moving, evolving system that caters to the needs of every learner.

From the classrooms of today, we will journey into the potential of tomorrow. Together, we will explore what the future could hold, guided by the central belief that education is, and must always be, a catalyst for transformation, a beacon of hope, and a promise of potential realized. So, buckle up as we take this leap into the future of education. Your presence, insights, and engagement are not just welcomed, they are essential. Onwards, to Chapter 11!

Chapter 11: The Road Ahead:

A Vision for the Future of Education

As we turn the page to the penultimate chapter of this narrative, we stand on the precipice of potential. The lessons of history and the victories of today have brought us to this vantage point, from where we look to the horizon with hope, armed with the question: What is our vision for the future of education?

Over the past few chapters, we've excavated the traditions that bind us and explored strategies that can foster growth in learning. But now, let's shift our gaze forward. Our ultimate goal is not merely to acknowledge the flaws of the current system or prescribe strategies for the present. It is to carve a path for an inclusive, empowering, and innovative future of education. How do we shape this future? What foundational pillars must we establish today to sustain this envisioned future?

- **Integration of Technology in Education:**

In the era of the fourth industrial revolution, technology has permeated every aspect of life, and education is no exception. From personalized learning algorithms to AI-driven educational tools, the potential of technology to revolutionize education is enormous. However, it's not about replacing teachers with technology; it's about using technology as a tool to enhance human elements in education. How can we weave technology seamlessly into the fabric of education, enhancing its reach, inclusivity, and efficacy?

In 2020, the global pandemic necessitated a sudden shift to online education, exposing the stark digital divide. However, it also highlighted the potential of digital platforms to democratize education (Reich et al., 2020). Imagine a future where a child in a remote village has access to the same quality of education as a child in a metropolitan city, facilitated by robust digital infrastructure and equitable access policies. But, this brings us to another critical question: How can we bridge the digital divide to ensure that the benefits of technology-enhanced education are accessible to all?

1. **Creating a Culture of Lifelong Learning:**

In a rapidly evolving world, the ability to learn, unlearn, and relearn is paramount (Toffler, 1970). Our education system should inculcate the spirit of lifelong learning, fostering curiosity, critical thinking, and a growth mindset. What strategies can schools adopt to cultivate these essential life skills? How can we make learning a joyous journey rather than a stressful sprint towards scores and grades?

Consider the story of an experimental school in Scandinavia that eliminated the concept of 'grades'. Instead, they focused on comprehensive feedback and a growth-oriented approach. Teachers observed that students were more engaged, collaborative, and displayed a significant improvement in their understanding of concepts (Lundahl and Folke, 2016). Can such models be our stepping-stones towards a future where education is not a competitive race but a journey of growth and self-discovery?

1. Preparing for the Jobs of the Future:

The World Economic Forum reports that 65% of children entering primary school today will end up working in jobs that don't yet exist (WEF, 2016). With AI and automation transforming the job market, it is critical to equip our students with skills like problem-solving, creativity, emotional intelligence, and adaptability, often referred to as '21st-century skills'. How can our education system evolve to cater to this changing landscape? How can we balance the need for foundational knowledge with the importance of these soft skills?

Case in point is a school district in Canada that introduced a curriculum focusing on problem-solving, creativity, and critical thinking. Instead of conventional tests, students undertook projects addressing real-world problems, and their progress was assessed based on their problem-solving approach and innovative solutions. Five years into this initiative, not only did students exhibit enhanced 21st-century skills, but their academic performance also improved (Fadel et al., 2017). Could this be a window into a future where education is about nurturing problem-solvers and innovators rather than mere repositories of information?

1. **Inclusive and Equitable Education:**

We have discussed the importance of inclusivity in education. However, achieving it in its truest sense is an ongoing challenge. It's not only about physical access but also about creating an environment where every child feels seen, heard, and valued. It's about recognizing and addressing systemic biases, ensuring every child has the opportunity to realize their full potential, irrespective of their race, gender, socioeconomic status, or ability. What systemic changes do we need to institute to make this a reality? How can we create an education system that is truly 'for all'?

A school in New Zealand offers us a glimpse into such a future. Embracing the Maori philosophy of 'ako', they transformed their pedagogy to be more reciprocal and respectful, fostering a culture of mutual learning between teachers and students. They also incorporated strategies to celebrate the cultural diversity of their students, making the learning environment more inclusive and enriching (Bishop et al., 2014). Could such a model be our beacon as we sail towards a future where every learner finds a place of belonging in the education system?

1. **Further Integration of Technology in Education:**

In 2022, a tech giant introduced an AI-powered learning platform that uses machine learning algorithms to provide personalized learning experiences, adapting to the learner's pace and learning style (West, 2022). Students interact with the platform through voice commands, which helps foster communication skills. This example of innovative edtech application points to a promising direction. But a crucial question persists: How can we ensure such technology is used ethically and responsibly to enhance learning while preserving human interaction and social learning?

Another case study worth noting is the 'One Laptop per Child' initiative in Uruguay (Plan Ceibal, 2007). The program aimed to reduce the digital divide by providing every student with a laptop and internet connection. The project reached 100% coverage in 2009 and reported positive impacts on learning outcomes. This is a robust case for investing in digital infrastructure and equitable access to technology in education.

1. **Cultivating a Culture of Lifelong Learning:**

The Australian Education Department's "Alice Springs (Mparntwe) Education Declaration" provides an exemplary framework for fostering lifelong learning (Education Council, 2019). The policy emphasizes nurturing curiosity and creativity, promoting a culture of inquiry and innovation in classrooms. How can other countries adapt such frameworks in their context?

1. **Preparation for Future Jobs:**

Project-based learning is a potent strategy to nurture 21st-century skills. High Tech High, a network of charter schools in San Diego, operates entirely on a project-based curriculum (Rosenstock & Martinez, 2019). Students work on real-world projects, collaborating with peers and learning by doing. The school reports enhanced student engagement, creativity, and problem-solving abilities.

1. **Achieving Inclusive and Equitable Education:**

The practice of Universal Design for Learning (UDL) is an effective approach to making education more inclusive. The UDL framework proposes that learning environments and materials should be flexible and adaptable to accommodate all learners' diverse needs (CAST, 2018). Schools implementing UDL have reported positive impacts on student engagement, understanding, and performance.

A comprehensive case study of inclusive education is the Finnish education system (Sahlberg, 2015).

Finland ensures quality education for all students, regardless of their background or abilities, through policies like qualified teachers for all schools, personalized learning plans, and no tracking until high school. Finnish students consistently perform well in international assessments, and the system has negligible disparities in learning outcomes across schools.

As we have journeyed through the pages of this chapter, we have sketched out an ambitious but achievable vision for the future of education. We have seen how further integration of technology can provide personalized learning experiences and bridge the digital divide, as evidenced by initiatives like AI-powered learning platforms and Uruguay's 'One Laptop per Child' program.

We've recognized the need to cultivate a culture of lifelong learning, as championed by Australia's "Alice Springs (Mparntwe) Education Declaration," and the importance of preparing students for future jobs through methods like project-based learning implemented at High Tech High.

In our quest for inclusivity and equity, we've explored the Universal Design for Learning and admired the Finnish education system's successful practices in inclusive education. As we look ahead, we must remember that our journey is complex, and the transformation we seek will require collective will and systemic change.

This vision for the future of education is not just a dream; it's a mandate. In our concluding chapter, we issue a 'Call to Arms.' It's time for all of us - educators, policymakers, parents, and students - to embrace our role in this grand transformation. The future of education is not a destination we passively await but a reality we actively create. Let's forge ahead into our final chapter, ready to take up the mantle and transform education for all.

Chapter 12: Conclusion - A Call to Arms:

Embracing Our Role in Transforming Education

Education isn't just a pathway to personal growth and career opportunities. It's a tool to shape society, a means of crafting the world of tomorrow. This essential principle has been reiterated time and again throughout this book, taking us on a journey from antiquity to the future, investigating how education has evolved, pinpointing the flaws and successes, and offering a vision for the years ahead.

Now, we reach the end, and yet, it isn't an end at all but a beginning. It's a call to arms for every educator, policymaker, parent, student, and citizen. We must realize the crucial part we all play in shaping education and, by extension, society. Here, we'll explore key questions, provide answers based on our journey so far, and offer a final case study that exemplifies the spirit of this conclusion.

1. Why should I care about educational transformation?

Every aspect of our lives is impacted by education. As Nelson Mandela famously stated, "Education is the most powerful weapon which you can use to change the world." An investment in education isn't just personal but collective. It affects economic prosperity, social mobility, and societal harmony. Therefore, everyone, regardless of their occupation or background, has a vested interest in ensuring the education system functions optimally (Murnane & Levy, 1996).

2.Can education truly be a catalyst for societal transformation?

Education plays a vital role in driving societal change. It's a tool for addressing inequalities, cultivating informed citizens, and driving innovation. The more inclusive, equitable, and high-quality our education systems are, the better the prospects for societal growth (UNESCO, 2022). The example of Finland's education transformation, which has led to it being one of the most educationally successful countries, illustrates this point.

1. What role do teachers play in this transformation?

Teachers are on the frontline of educational change. They're not just dispensers of knowledge but are instrumental in shaping learning environments, fostering critical thinking, and nurturing curiosity. Teachers have the capacity to ignite a love for learning, foster resilience, and help students realize their potential. They also play a significant role in implementing educational reforms and innovations (Darling-Hammond & Adamson, 2010).

4 How can technology and AI contribute to this transformation?
Technology and AI have immense potential in revolutionizing education. They can personalize learning, increase accessibility, foster global collaboration, and equip students with 21st-century skills. However, their implementation needs to be thoughtful, informed by pedagogical insights and focused on enhancing human capacities (Schwab, 2016).

1. What strategies can foster growth in learning?

A myriad of strategies can be employed, but some common themes emerge. These include active learning, collaborative learning, critical thinking, differentiated instruction, and a focus on skill-building alongside knowledge acquisition (Tomlinson & McTighe, 2006; Ericsson, Krampe, & Tesch-Römer, 1993). The utilization of technology for personalized learning and data-informed teaching also holds promise (Bill & Melinda Gates Foundation, 2015).

1. How can I contribute to this transformation?

Every person has a role to play. As educators, we can innovate within our classrooms, foster a love for learning, and advocate for systemic changes. Policymakers can craft policies that prioritize education and innovation. Parents can support their children's learning journeys and advocate for better educational practices. Even as students, we can take ownership of our learning, seek out knowledge, and leverage opportunities provided by technology.

Case study: Malala Yousafzai

Let's look at an ordinary citizen who made a remarkable impact on education. It wasn't a policy, a breakthrough in AI, or a seismic societal shift, but a single determined individual who created a ripple effect of change. This person is Malala Yousafzai.

Born in Pakistan, Malala believed in the power of education. When her right to education was threatened by the Taliban, she didn't back down; she spoke up. Despite an attempt on her life, Malala continued her fight, a battle that took her all the way to the United Nations. Today, she's a Nobel laureate and continues her fight for girls' education through the Malala Fund.

Her story, like many others we've explored, is a testament to the potential that lies in every individual to spark change. It's a call to each of us to embrace our roles in transforming education. As we continue this journey, remember that education is not a privilege, but a human right. Let us work together to ensure it serves as a powerful tool to unlock human potential, foster societal harmony, and shape the world of tomorrow.

Case Study: Singapore

When we ask why educational transformation matters, we need to look no further than the impacts of such transformations on a global scale. For instance, consider the case of Singapore, a country with limited natural resources but invested heavily in education after its independence in 1965. Today, it's renowned for having one of the world's highest-performing education systems (OECD, 2016). Its strategy included a strong emphasis on teacher training, a rigorous curriculum, and continuous innovation, demonstrating the tangible benefits of prioritizing education.

Case Study: Erin Gruwell

As for the role of teachers, let's consider the story of Erin Gruwell, immortalized in the film "Freedom Writers." Working in a racially divided school with students who faced tremendous challenges, Gruwell utilized unconventional teaching methods to inspire her students. Her story underscores the significant impact a single educator can have in transforming the lives of students (Gruwell, 1999).

Case Study: Khan Academy

The potential of technology and AI is perhaps best illustrated by the rise of Massive Open Online Courses (MOOCs) and platforms like Khan Academy, which have democratized access to high-quality education. Research from the Christensen Institute (2017) shows that these platforms have enabled millions of learners globally to acquire new skills and knowledge, often free of cost.

The strategies that can foster growth in learning are numerous and context-dependent. However, the flipped classroom model has gained popularity and shown effectiveness in various settings. It involves students engaging with course material independently and using classroom time for discussions, problem-solving, and personalized guidance. Research shows this model can enhance student engagement and outcomes (Bishop & Verleger, 2013).

Case Study: Sugata Mitra's Hole in the Wall

Everyone's contribution to this transformation is critical. Consider the story of Sugata Mitra's "Hole in the Wall" experiment.

Mitra installed a computer in a wall in a slum in New Delhi and left it for the local children to explore. With no direct instruction, the children learned to use the computer and even picked up English to better use the software. Mitra's experiment demonstrates the power of curiosity and self-directed learning, proving that everyone, regardless of their background, can contribute to and benefit from educational innovation (Mitra, 2010).

Chapter 12 marks the culmination of our exploration of the past, present, and future of education. We began by underscoring the profound influence of educational transformation on a global scale, highlighting Malala Yousafzai, Singapore's exceptional educational success and the inspirational story of teacher Erin Gruwell, whose unique teaching methods brought about life-altering change for her students.

We also emphasized the powerful potential of technology and AI in modern education, discussing how platforms like MOOCs and Khan Academy have democratized learning worldwide. Additionally, we delved into the flipped classroom model, a strategy demonstrating enhanced student engagement and outcomes.

One of the most compelling stories of this chapter was that of Sugata Mitra's "Hole in the Wall" experiment. It exemplified the extraordinary power of curiosity and self-directed learning, reminding us that everyone, regardless of their background, can contribute to educational innovation.

As we close this chapter and our exploration, we urge every reader to view education not as a mere system or policy but as a living, evolving entity shaped by our collective actions and beliefs.

We all have a role in transforming education into a formidable tool for societal advancement. The road ahead may be demanding, yet with a shared commitment and relentless curiosity, we can shape an educational future that is equitable, inclusive, and capable of unlocking humanity's full potential.

To everyone who's made it this far, take a moment to consider what you've learned, how it's made you feel, and what action it inspires you to take. After all, knowledge isn't merely for understanding—it's for doing. So, let's move forward, armed with the insights gathered and the conviction that change is possible. Let us embrace our role in transforming education for the better.

Chapter 13: Envisioning the Future:

A Blueprint for the AA STEM & Entrepreneurship Academy

In this pivotal moment in our history, as an advocate for education reform, lay before you a vision that has the potential to revolutionize our traditional notions of education. Imagine a world where schools don't just produce employees for companies, but a world where they create the future leaders of Fortune 500 companies.

Picture a school that fosters the next Elon Musk, Mark Zuckerberg, Jeff Bezos, Steve Jobs - visionaries who not only find their places in society but create places for others.

I present to you the blueprint of AA STEM & Entrepreneurship Academy. This institution, while not yet realized, embodies an audacious aspiration: to shift the focus from producing workers to developing thinkers, innovators, and entrepreneurs. This is an appeal to educators, politicians, and global citizens: join in transforming this vision into a reality, changing not just individual lives but the trajectory of our society.

The AA STEM & Entrepreneurship Academy intertwines the principles of Science, Technology, Engineering, and Math (STEM) with artistic creativity and production. It is a school that believes every child has unique gifts. Be it in music, sports, writing, or the arts - these talents are to be nurtured, not suppressed. The Academy aims to show students how these gifts can be used to benefit their communities and pave the way to a successful career path.

In this envisioned academy, learning transcends the traditional boundaries of classroom walls. It provides real-world experiences in science and math. Here, learning is a process that kindles curiosity and brings knowledge to life. Students are not passive consumers of information; they are creators, thinkers, problem solvers, and future leaders.

The envisioned academy also instills an entrepreneurial mindset in students. They are not merely being prepared for the workforce; they are being groomed to shape it. Their artistic talents transform into tools for change, platforms for service, and potential enterprises. These students are equipped to solve problems within their communities and beyond, taking the first steps on a journey towards future leadership.

Moreover, this proposed academy emphasizes collaboration. Students learn to harness their unique gifts in concert, creating a collaborative environment that fosters innovation. They are encouraged to offer their skills to small businesses, creating symbiotic relationships that benefit the students, the school, and the community.

Such a blueprint is audacious but necessary. The AA STEM & Entrepreneurship Academy embodies a paradigm shift in education. This vision aims not only to reform but revolutionize the purpose of education: it should be about self-discovery, community service, and innovation. It emphasizes the importance of students creating their own paths to success, rather than following a predetermined route.

The impact of realizing this vision extends beyond the walls of the Academy. This is a call to action for everyone: educators, to explore and adopt innovative teaching methods; politicians, to support policies that foster creativity and entrepreneurial spirit; and community members, to embrace and nurture the potential in every child.

This vision, while ambitious, is achievable. We stand on the cusp of an educational revolution that could create a generation of thinkers and creators, rather than mere workers. With your help, we can turn this vision into a reality. Together, we can change the narrative of education, shaping not only our future but the future of generations to come.

Join me on this journey. Together, let us make the AA STEM & Entrepreneurship Academy a reality and herald a new dawn in education. Together, let us ignite change and shape a world where every child is not just equipped for the future, but is empowered to create it.

Appendix

Lesson Plan Examples

Lesson Title: Building Bridges: An Exercise in Engineering and Teamwork
Grade Level: 5th grade, adaptable for 2nd grade

Learning Objective:

- To understand the basic principles of bridge construction and engineering.
- To demonstrate teamwork and collaboration in completing a hands-on task.

Learning Target:

- I can explain the principles of bridge construction.
- I can work effectively in a team to build a bridge that supports a specific weight.

Materials Needed:

- Popsicle sticks
- White glue
- Weights (can use coins or small objects)

Duration: 90 minutes

Lesson Procedure:

Step 1: Introduction (15 minutes) Begin by introducing the concept of engineering and bridge construction. Discuss the purpose of a bridge and the considerations an engineer must make when designing a bridge, such as materials, location, and load-bearing capacity. Tailor the depth of this conversation to fit the grade level. For younger students, keep the concepts simple.

Step 2: Group Formation and Instructions (10 minutes) Divide the class into small groups of about 3-4 students each. Explain the challenge: each group is to use the provided materials (Popsicle sticks and glue) to build a bridge that can support as much weight as possible.

Step 3: Bridge Building (45 minutes) Allow groups to begin planning and building their bridges. Circulate around the room to facilitate and answer questions. Ensure all students are participating. For younger students, you might suggest a simple bridge design to get them started.

Step 4: Testing (10 minutes) After the bridges are built, allow the glue to dry if needed. Then, test each bridge by gradually adding weight (like coins) until the bridge collapses. Make this a fun and exciting event, and be sure to celebrate the effort, not just the result.

Step 5: Reflection (10 minutes) Lead a discussion about the process. Ask questions like:

- What designs were most successful, and why?
- What would you do differently next time?
- How did your team work together? What strategies did you use?

Homework Assignment: Have students draw a picture of their bridge and write a paragraph about what they learned from the activity. For younger students, the paragraph could be just a few sentences.

Tips for Adaptation for 2nd Graders:

- Simplify the engineering concepts during the introduction, focusing on the purpose of a bridge and what makes it strong (like triangle shapes in the design).
- You might demonstrate a simple bridge design to get them started.
- During reflection, focus on teamwork and simple observations about what made the bridges strong or weak. Ask them to share their favorite part of building the bridge.

The proposed lesson plan primarily supports the following chapters in the book:

1. **Chapter 3: Experimental Learning: The Beacon of Transformation in Education**: This lesson plan emphasizes hands-on, experimental learning. Students are not passively receiving information, but actively constructing knowledge through building and testing their bridges. The bridge-building activity provides a tangible experience that anchors abstract engineering concepts, demonstrating the transformational power of experimental learning.

2. **Chapter 5: Shaping the Learning Landscape: The Role of Today's Educators in Transformation**: The role of the teacher in this lesson is that of a facilitator who guides students through the process, encouraging exploration, teamwork, and problem-solving. This aligns with the chapter's focus on how educators can shape learning experiences to foster deeper understanding and engagement.

3. **Chapter 7: Nurturing Innovation: Building a Culture of Creativity and Learning**: The open-ended nature of the task promotes innovation and creativity. Students are not given a single "right" way to build their bridge, fostering an environment where creativity is valued and innovative solutions are encouraged.

4. **Chapter 9: Unleashing Potential: Strategies to Foster Growth in Learning**: By working in teams, students have the opportunity to develop and practice important collaborative skills. Furthermore, the process of designing, building, and testing the bridge helps students learn from failure and success, promoting growth.

The rationale behind this alignment is that the lesson plan is designed to create an active, engaging, and collaborative learning environment that promotes creativity, problem-solving, and deeper understanding. These are key aspects highlighted in the above chapters as crucial for transforming education and fostering effective learning.

Lesson 2: Exploring Ecosystems: Hands-on Learning in Life Science

Grade Level: 5th Grade (adaptable for 2nd graders)
Subject: Science

Learning Objective: Students will be able to understand the components of an ecosystem, including the roles of producers, consumers, and decomposers.

Learning Target: By the end of the lesson, students will be able to define an ecosystem and describe how producers, consumers, and decomposers interact within an ecosystem.

Materials:

1. Chart paper
2. Markers
3. Online resources or books about ecosystems
4. Craft supplies: construction paper, scissors, glue, magazines (for pictures of plants, animals, etc.)
5. Mini ecosystem kits (terrarium or aquarium if available)

Procedure:

1. **Introduction (15 minutes):** Begin the lesson by asking students what they know about ecosystems. Write their ideas on the chart paper. Then, provide a simple definition of an ecosystem. Discuss the roles of producers (plants), consumers

(animals), and decomposers (like fungi or bacteria) in an ecosystem.

2. **Group Work - Ecosystem Research (30 minutes):** Divide the students into small groups and assign each group an ecosystem to research (like a forest, a desert, an ocean, etc.). Each group will use online resources or books to learn about the producers, consumers, and decomposers in their assigned ecosystem. Guide them to identify how these components interact in their specific ecosystem.

3. **Creating Ecosystem Collages (30 minutes):** Using their research, each group will create a collage that represents their assigned ecosystem. They should include pictures or drawings of different producers, consumers, and decomposers, and visually demonstrate the interactions between them.

4. **Presentations and Discussions (10 minutes):** Each group will present their collage, explaining what their ecosystem is, what producers, consumers, and decomposers are present, and how they interact. After each presentation, allow for questions and discussion.

5. **Reflection (5 minutes):** At the end of the lesson, revisit the chart from the beginning of the class. Have students add to or correct their initial ideas based on what they learned during the lesson.

Adaptation for 2nd Graders: For younger students, you may need to simplify the language and concepts. Instead of dividing into small groups, conduct the research portion as a whole class activity, choosing one simple ecosystem (like a forest) to explore. During the collage activity, guide them in creating a class collage on a large piece of chart paper, where each student adds one element to the ecosystem.

The lesson on exploring ecosystems and understanding the roles of different components within the system can be connected to the following chapters in the book:

1. **Chapter 3: Experimental Learning: The Beacon of Transformation in Education** - This lesson plan supports this chapter as it promotes experimental learning. By researching different ecosystems and creating a visual representation of what they've learned, students are actively engaged in experimental learning. They're not just passively receiving information; they're actively seeking it out, processing it, and using it in a hands-on way.

Rationale: The active, hands-on exploration of ecosystems allows students to learn experientially, rather than through mere memorization or passive reception of information. The collaborative nature of the activities also promotes social learning.

1. **Chapter 7: Nurturing Innovation: Building a Culture of Creativity and Learning** - This lesson fosters creativity and innovation through the task of creating an ecosystem collage. The students are not only learning about ecosystems, but they're also using their creative skills to visualize and represent their learning.

Rationale: Engaging students in creative tasks aids in enhancing their ability to think innovatively, to represent their learning in unique ways, and to appreciate the creative process. This also aids in building a culture of creativity and innovation in the classroom.

1. **Chapter 9: Unleashing Potential: Strategies to Foster Growth in Learning** - The group work, presentations, and discussions in this lesson are strategies that can foster growth in learning. Students can deepen their understanding by hearing about different ecosystems from their peers, and they can improve their communication skills by presenting their work to the class.

Rationale: Giving students the opportunity to work in groups, conduct research, and present their findings allows them to develop a wide range of skills, including collaboration, communication, research, and critical thinking. These are all skills that foster growth in learning and prepare students for future educational and career endeavors.

1. **Chapter 10: Education for All: Making Change Inclusive and Accessible** - By allowing students to research and present on different ecosystems, we are creating an inclusive educational experience. This lesson plan can be easily adapted to cater to students of different learning levels and styles.

Rationale: It's important to design lessons that are accessible and inclusive, ensuring that all students have the opportunity to learn and succeed. This lesson plan meets those goals by offering various ways for students to engage with the material, allowing for different learning styles and preferences.

Lesson Plan 3: Harnessing AI and Technology (Chapter 4)
Title: "Creating with Code: An Introduction to Programming"

Grade Level: 2nd-5th grade (Adaptable)
Objective:

- Students will be introduced to the basics of coding and programming.
- Students will develop problem-solving and logical thinking skills.
- Students will gain an understanding of the role of coding in the digital age.

Learning Target: I can use an online platform to create and solve coding puzzles or complete a coding project.

Materials Needed:

- Computers or tablets with internet access
- Online coding platform (e.g., Code.org, Scratch, Tynker)

Lesson Steps:
Introduction (10 minutes)

- Begin the lesson by discussing the importance of coding in today's world. Explain how coding is used in various technologies, such as apps, websites, and robots.

- Engage students in a brief discussion about their experiences with technology and how they think coding is involved in creating those technologies.

Activity: Guided Coding (60 minutes)

- Introduce the online coding platform you have chosen for the lesson (e.g., Code.org, Scratch, Tynker). Explain that they will be using this platform to learn and practice coding skills.
- Demonstrate the basic features and tools of the platform, such as how to drag and drop blocks of code, create characters or animations, and interact with the program.
- Start with a series of coding puzzles or a guided project available on the platform. Walk students through each step, explaining concepts and providing examples.
- Encourage students to think critically and problem-solve as they encounter challenges. Emphasize the importance of perseverance and learning from mistakes.

Reflection and Sharing (20 minutes)

- After completing the coding activity, gather students together for a group discussion.
- Ask students to reflect on their experience and share any challenges they faced while coding. Prompt them to discuss how they overcame those challenges.
- Facilitate a discussion about the skills they used during the coding activity, such as problem-solving, logical thinking, and creativity.
- Encourage students to share their creations or achievements from the coding activity, allowing them to showcase their work and inspire their peers.

To adapt the "Creating with Code: An Introduction to Programming" lesson for 2nd graders, it's important to simplify the concepts and adjust the activities to match their developmental level. Here's a suggested adaptation:

Title: "Exploring Patterns: Introduction to Sequencing and Patterns with Coding" Objective: To introduce 2nd-grade students to basic concepts of sequencing and patterns using a simplified coding activity.

Introduction:

1. Begin by discussing the importance of following sequences and recognizing patterns in everyday life, such as following a recipe or identifying patterns in nature.

Activity:

1. Use a simplified coding platform suitable for young learners, such as Code.org's "Blockly" or "ScratchJr."
2. Introduce the basic commands and coding blocks, such as forward, backward, turn left, and turn right.
3. Guide students through a hands-on activity where they create a sequence of commands to move a character or object on the screen.
4. Start with simple sequences, like making the character move forward three times and then turn right.
5. Gradually introduce the concept of patterns by asking students to identify and replicate simple patterns in their code, such as repeating a sequence.

6. Encourage creativity by allowing students to customize their characters or backgrounds.

Reflection:

1. After the coding activity, engage students in a discussion about their experience.
2. Ask students about the patterns they observed and how they used sequencing to achieve specific outcomes.
3. Encourage them to share any challenges they faced and how they overcame them.

Adapting the lesson for 2nd graders:

1. Simplify the coding platform: Use age-appropriate platforms like Code.org's "Blockly" or "ScratchJr" that offer a more visual and intuitive interface.
2. Focus on basic commands: Limit the available coding blocks to essential commands like moving forward, turning, and repeating actions.
3. Provide scaffolding: Offer step-by-step guidance and support as students navigate the coding platform.
4. Use familiar contexts: Frame the coding activities around familiar scenarios or themes that resonate with 2nd graders, such as guiding a character through a maze or creating a dance routine.

By adapting the lesson in this way, you make it more accessible and engaging for 2nd graders while still introducing them to the fundamental concepts of sequencing and patterns through coding.

Rationale: Including the "Creating with Code" lesson plan provides an opportunity to showcase how coding and programming can be integrated into various aspects of education. By connecting it to chapters that explore experimental learning, nurturing innovation, and strategies for growth, the lesson plan demonstrates the practical application and relevance of coding in transforming education. It highlights the connection between coding and the broader themes discussed throughout the book, promoting a holistic understanding of how technology can shape the future of education.

The lesson plan for "Creating with Code: An Introduction to Programming" can also be connected to the following chapters:

1. Chapter 4: "The Digital Age: Harnessing the Power of AI and Technology in Education." By introducing students to coding and programming, it aligns with the chapter's focus on utilizing technology as a powerful educational tool. The lesson aims to equip students with foundational coding skills, promoting computational thinking, problem-solving, and creativity. By providing an interactive and engaging learning experience, students can begin to understand the possibilities and potential of technology in shaping their future.
2. Chapter 3: Experimental Learning: The Beacon of Transformation in Education

    - Experimental learning often involves hands-on activities and interactive experiences, which aligns with the active and engaging nature of coding and programming. Both experimental learning and coding emphasize the importance of learning by doing and exploring new concepts.

1. Chapter 7: Nurturing Innovation: Building a Culture of Creativity and Learning

- Coding and programming require creativity and innovative thinking. By introducing students to coding, educators can foster a culture of creativity and innovation in the classroom. This chapter explores strategies for nurturing and promoting creativity, making it relevant to the coding lesson.

1. Chapter 9: Unleashing Potential: Strategies to Foster Growth in Learning

- Coding encourages students to develop problem-solving skills, critical thinking, and perseverance. These strategies for fostering growth in learning align with the goals of Chapter 9. Coding empowers students to think critically, analyze problems, and develop creative solutions.

Lesson 4 Title: Exploring Cultural Diversity: Celebrating Our Differences
Subject Social Studies.
Learning Objective: Students will understand and appreciate cultural diversity by exploring different traditions and celebrations from around the world.
Learning Target: I can investigate and share information about different cultural traditions and celebrations, recognizing and appreciating the diversity of our global community.
Materials:

- World map or globe
- Chart paper or whiteboard
- Markers or colored pencils
- Laptops, tablets, or access to the internet
- Construction paper
- Scissors and glue
- Art supplies (e.g., crayons, colored pencils, markers)

Procedure:

1. **Warm-up (10 minutes):** Begin by showing students a world map or globe. Engage them in a discussion about different countries and cultures. Ask questions such as:

- What do you know about different countries and cultures around the world?

- Can you name any traditions or celebrations from other countries?
- Why is it important to learn about different cultures?

1. **Introduction (5 minutes)**: Explain to students that they will be exploring different cultural traditions and celebrations from around the world. Share the learning objective and learning target to provide clarity.
2. **Research (30 minutes)**:

- Divide students into small groups and assign each group a different country or cultural tradition to research (e.g., Diwali in India, Chinese New Year, Day of the Dead in Mexico).
- Provide laptops, tablets, or access to the internet for students to conduct their research. Encourage them to gather information about the significance, customs, and rituals associated with the assigned tradition or celebration.
- Remind students to take notes and gather visuals (pictures, videos) that represent the tradition or celebration.

1. **Collaborative Sharing (20 minutes)**:

- Bring the students back together and have each group share their findings with the class. Encourage students to use visuals and explain the significance of the traditions or celebrations they researched.
- As a class, create a chart or a mind map on chart paper or the whiteboard to record the key information learned about each tradition or celebration.

1. **Artistic Representation (20 minutes)**:

- Distribute construction paper, scissors, glue, and art supplies to each student.
- Instruct students to choose one of the traditions or celebrations discussed and create a colorful poster or artwork that represents it.
- Encourage students to be creative and use symbols, colors, and images that capture the essence of the tradition or celebration.

1. **Reflection and Discussion (15 minutes):**

- Once students have completed their artwork, ask them to reflect on what they have learned and how it has influenced their understanding of cultural diversity.
- Lead a class discussion by asking questions such as:
    - What did you find most interesting about the traditions or celebrations you researched?
    - How does learning about different cultures help us appreciate diversity?
    - Why is it important to respect and celebrate cultural differences?

1. **Wrap-up (5 minutes):** Summarize the key takeaways from the lesson and emphasize the importance of embracing and respecting cultural diversity.

Extension Activity: Encourage students to share their artwork and what they learned with their families or friends. They can write a short paragraph describing the tradition or celebration they depicted in their artwork and why it is meaningful to them.

Adaptations for 2nd Grade:

- Simplify the research portion by providing pre-selected information about each tradition or celebration for students to explore.
- Use age-appropriate language and visuals to explain the significance of cultural diversity.
- Provide additional guidance and support during the art activity to ensure success for younger students.
- Modify the reflection and discussion questions to suit the developmental level of 2nd graders.

This lesson supports several chapters in the book, "Igniting Change: A New Dawn in the Cyclical World of Education." Here is the rationale for each chapter:

1. Chapter 5: Shaping the Learning Landscape: The Role of Today's Educators in Transformation

    - This lesson promotes cultural awareness and appreciation, which aligns with the educator's role in creating an inclusive and diverse learning environment.

1. Chapter 7: Nurturing Innovation: Building a Culture of Creativity and Learning.

By encouraging students to explore different cultural traditions and express their understanding through artwork, this lesson fosters creativity and innovation.

1. Chapter 10: Education for All: Making Change Inclusive and Accessible

- The lesson promotes inclusivity by highlighting and celebrating cultural diversity. It encourages students to recognize and respect differences, promoting a more inclusive educational experience.

1. Chapter 11: The Road Ahead: A Vision for the Future of Education

- This lesson aligns with the vision for the future of education by emphasizing global citizenship, cultural competence, and the importance of embracing diversity in an increasingly interconnected world.

References

Arnett, T. (2019). The Promise of AI for Personalizing Learning. Clayton Christensen Institute.

Bacon, F. (1620). Novum Organum Scientiarum ('New Instrument of Science').

Bell, S. (2010). Project-based learning for the 21st century: Skills for the future. The Clearing House, 83(2), 39-43.

Black, P., & Wiliam, D. (1998). Assessment and classroom learning. Assessment in Education: Principles, Policy & Practice, 5(1), 7-74.

Bostrom, N. (2014). Superintelligence: Paths, Dangers, Strategies. Oxford University Press.

Boaler, J. (2002). Experiencing school mathematics: Traditional and reform approaches to teaching and their impact on student learning. Lawrence Erlbaum Associates.

Cheung, A. C., & Slavin, R. E. (2013). The effectiveness of educational technology applications for enhancing mathematics achievement in K-12 classrooms: A meta-analysis. Educational Research Review, 9, 88–113.

Christensen, C., Horn, M. & Johnson, C. (2008). Disrupting Class: How Disruptive Innovation Will Change the Way the World Learns. McGraw-Hill Education.

Collins, J. (2001). Good to Great: Why Some Companies Make the Leap... and Others Don't. HarperBusiness.

Csikszentmihalyi, M. (1996). Creativity: Flow and the Psychology of Discovery and Invention. HarperCollins.

Darling-Hammond, L. (2017). Empowered Educators: How High-Performing Systems Shape Teaching Quality Around the World. Jossey-Bass.

Darling-Hammond, L., & Richardson, N. (2009). Research review/teacher learning: What matters? Educational Leadership, 66(5), 46–53.

Davis, J. (2003). Early Childhood Environmental Education: Making it Mainstream. Early Childhood Australia.
Deloitte Access Economics. (2018). Soft skills for business success. Deloitte Access Economics.

Dweck, C. S. (2006). Mindset: The new psychology of success. Random House.

Dweck, C. S. (2007). Mindset: The New Psychology of Success. Ballantine Books.

Ertmer, P. A., & Ottenbreit-Leftwich, A. T. (2010). Teacher Technology Change: How Knowledge, Confidence, Beliefs, and Culture Intersect. Journal of Research on Technology in Education, 42(3), 255–284.

Fink, L. Dee (2013). Creating Significant Learning Experiences: An Integrated Approach to Designing College Courses. San Francisco, CA: Jossey-Bass.

Fullan, M. (2001). Leading in a Culture of Change. Jossey-Bass.

Fullan, M. (2011). The Moral Imperative Realized. Corwin.

Gleason, B., & von Gillern, S. (2018). Digital citizenship with social media: Participatory practices of teaching and learning in secondary education. Educational Technology & Society, 21(1), 200–212.

Heritage, M. (2010). Formative assessment: Making it happen in the classroom. Thousand Oaks, CA: Corwin Press.

Jobs, S. (1996). Triumph of the Nerds: The Rise of Accidental Empires. (Documentary). PBS.

Johnson, D. W., & Johnson, R. T. (1999). Making Cooperative Learning Work. Theory into Practice, 38(2), 67–73.

Johnson, D. W., & Johnson, R. T. (2009). An educational psychology success story: Social interdependence theory and cooperative learning. Educational Researcher, 38(5), 365–379.

Kolb, D. A. (1984). Experiential learning: Experience as the source of learning and development (Vol. 1). Englewood Cliffs, NJ: Prentice-Hall.

Kotter, J. P. (1996). Leading Change. Harvard Business School Press.
Loreman, T., Deppeler, J., & Harvey, D. (2011). Inclusive education: Supporting diversity in the classroom. Routledge.

Luckin, R. (2017). Towards Artificial Intelligence-Based Assessment Systems. Nature Human Behaviour, 1(3).

Mitra, D. L. (2008). Student Voice in School Reform: Reframing Student-Teacher Relationships. McGill Journal of Education, 43(1), 61-80.

Pane, J. F., Steiner, E. D., Baird, M. D., & Hamilton, L. S. (2015). Continued progress: Promising evidence on personalized learning. Santa Monica, CA: RAND Corporation.
Perkins, D. (2010). Making Learning Whole: How Seven Principles of Teaching Can Transform Education. Jossey-Bass.

Prensky, M. (2001). Digital natives, digital immigrants. On the Horizon, 9(5), 1–6.
Resnick, M. (2007). All I Really Need to Know (About Creative Thinking) I Learned (By Studying How Children Learn) in Kindergarten. Proceedings of the 6th ACM SIGCHI Conference on Creativity & Cognition, 1–6.

Robinson, K. (2001). Out of Our Minds: Learning to Be Creative. Capstone.

Rock, M. L., Gregg, M., Ellis, E., & Gable, R. A. (2008). REACH: A framework for differentiating classroom instruction. Preventing School Failure

Senge, P. (1990). The Fifth Discipline: The Art & Practice of The Learning Organization. Doubleday/Currency.

Tomlinson, C. A. (2001). How to differentiate instruction in mixed-ability classrooms. ASCD.

Tomlinson, C. A., & Imbeau, M. B. (2010). Leading and Managing a Differentiated Classroom. ASCD.

Towards Inclusive Education for All. UNESCO. 2005.

Tyack, D., & Cuban, L. (1995). Tinkering Toward Utopia: A Century of Public School Reform. Harvard University Press.

Weimer, M. (2002). Learner-centered teaching: Five key changes to practice. Jossey-Bass.

Weller, M. (2020). 25 Years of Ed Tech. Athabasca University Press.
Wooldridge, M. (2020). Artificial Intelligence: Structures and Strategies for Complex Problem Solving. Pearson Education.

World Economic Forum. (2020). The Future of Jobs Report 2020. World Economic Forum.

Xie, H., Chu, H. C., Hwang, G. J., & Wang, C. C. (2019). Trends and development in technology-enhanced adaptive/personalized learning: A systematic review of journal publications from 2007 to 2017. Computers & Education, 140.

York-Barr, J., & Duke, K. (2004). What Do We Know About Teacher Leadership? Findings From Two Decades of Scholarship. Review of Educational Research, 74(3), 255–316.

Zimmerman, B. J. (2000). Attaining self-regulation: A social cognitive perspective. In M. Boekaerts, P. R. Pintrich, & M. Zeidner (Eds.), Handbook of self-regulation (p. 13–39). Academic Press.

About the Author

Dr. Anton Anthony, Ed. S, ThD has served in school districts throughout Georgia as a teacher, discipline coordinator, coach, assistant principal, and principal.

He has worked in poverty-stricken schools where most of the population was Title I. He has also worked in schools where parents were highly educated, high-income professionals and business owners. Each school brought its own challenges, but he was able to break through barriers and achieve academic improvement everywhere he went.

Credentials

Dr. Anthony received his Bachelor of Arts with Honors in Business Management from Fort Valley State University in Georgia. He received his Masters of Arts in Teaching at Augusta State University. He later returned to receive a degree in Curriculum and Instruction from Augusta University and received his Educational Specialist add-on in Educational Leadership and Administration, also at Augusta University. He holds his Doctorate in Theology from North Central Theological Seminary. He is a licensed educator and real estate broker with the State of Georgia.

Career

He began his educational career as a reading specialist in Burke County, Georgia schools. He was moved into the 7th grade English/Language Arts program (ELA), where he experienced his first real taste of educational success. His class achieved the highest passing percentage, and he was given an award to recognize his achievement.

After spending a second year at the middle school where he began his career, he asked for a position as a coach at an alternative school in that same district. Former teacher of the year for the school, he was allowed to become the coach, discipline coordinator, and reading instructor.

From those positions, he would become an assistant principal and principal. He is currently a public school principal in Georgia to be closer to his children.

Current Status

Mr. Anthony currently lives in Georgia. He is a public school principal and one of the most active administrators on social media and looks forward to bringing his vision of AA STEAM & Entrepreneurship Academy to life.

Contact Information

To connect with Mr. Anthony online, you can find him online.
Facebook: http://facebook.com/anton.anthony1

Twitter:

https://Twitter.com/antonanthony5

Instagram:

Instagram.com/authorantonanthony

LinkedIn:

www.linkedin.com/in/authorantonanthonysr

YouTube:

https://www.youtube.com/channel/UCI77nqy8OXItxQ_ZazNSm0w

Email:

AAStemAcademy@gmail.com

antonanthonysr@gmail.com

contact@authorantonanthony.com

Phone: 706-799-2684

www.ingramcontent.com/pod-product-compliance
Lightning Source LLC
Chambersburg PA
CBHW050441010526
44118CB00013B/1626